MISSION TO MARS

HUMANS TO MARS

BY

JOHN HAMILTON

Abdo & Daughters
An imprint of Abdo Publishing | abdopublishing.com

abdopublishing.com

Published by Abdo Publishing, a division of ABDO, PO Box 398166, Minneapolis, Minnesota 55439. Copyright © 2019 by Abdo Consulting Group, Inc. International copyrights reserved in all countries. No part of this book may be reproduced in any form without written permission from the publisher. Abdo & Daughters™ is a trademark and logo of Abdo Publishing.

Printed in the United States of America, North Mankato, Minnesota.
072018
092018

Editor: Sue Hamilton
Copy Editor: Bridget O'Brien
Graphic Design: Sue Hamilton
Cover Design: Candice Keimig and Pakou Moua
Cover Photo: iStock
Interior Images: All Images NASA, except: 20th Century Fox-pgs 8-9; AP-pg 29; Bigelow Aerospace-pg 24; Chris Hadfield-pg 28; Dava Newman-pg 33; European Space Agency-pg 45 (Mars Express); Indian Space Research Organisation-pg 45 (Mars Orbiter Mission); National Geographic-pgs 12, 20-21, 26-27 & 42-43; Pacific Domes-pg 11 (bottom); Shutterstock-pgs 6-7, 25 & 41; SpaceX-pg 16.

Library of Congress Control Number: 2017963903
Publisher's Cataloging-in-Publication Data
Names: Hamilton, John, author.
Title: Humans to Mars / by John Hamilton
Description: Minneapolis, Minnesota : Abdo Publishing, 2019. | Series: Mission to Mars | Includes online resources and index.
Identifiers: ISBN 9781532115929 (lib.bdg.) | ISBN 9781532156854 (ebook)
Subjects: LCSH: Space travel--Juvenile literature. | Interplanetary voyages--Juvenile literature. | Space flight to Mars--Juvenile literature. | Mars (Planet)--Exploration--Juvenile literature.
Classification: DDC 523.43--dc23

CONTENTS

THE LURE OF THE RED PLANET

For centuries, people have gazed at Mars, that bright red dot in the night sky, and wondered if there were aliens there. Were they like us? Could we learn from each other? Or maybe the aliens were hostile. Maybe they were monsters bent on our destruction. Mars has been the subject of hundreds of science fiction tales, including books and movies. From *The War of the Worlds* to *The Martian*, these stories have set our imaginations on fire.

In the last several decades, the United States and a handful of other countries have sent a fleet of orbiters, landers, and rovers to Mars. We've learned much about the Red Planet. No longer a place of pure imagination, Mars is a real place that we can explore. As our knowledge and technology grows, the question naturally arises: can people someday set foot on Mars? Can we live and work there in cities? Is it possible to transform that hostile, alien planet so that it is like our own Earth?

These questions are no longer flights of fancy. We have the desire and the technology to colonize Mars. The journey will be filled with danger, and there are many problems to be solved. Despite the hard road ahead, scientists around the world today are working to solve these roadblocks. The future is now.

CAN HUMANS LIVE ON MARS?

The first question we need to answer about building colonies on Mars is: can humans even live on that remote, forbidding planet? "Absolutely," says Jim Green, a chief scientist at NASA. Green points out that recent discoveries show there is a good chance Mars once harbored life. In fact, microscopic life may live there today.

Probes sent to Mars, such as NASA's Mars Reconnaissance Orbiter and Curiosity rover, have uncovered clues about the planet's ability to support living things. There is much water ice buried under the Martian surface and at the poles. Water is a crucial ingredient for all life as we know it. Mars was once filled with oceans of liquid water. The proof is in the canyons and dried lakes and rivers we can observe today from orbit. Perhaps all that water helped life spring forth, much as it did on Earth.

In fact, there may be microbial life thriving underground on Mars today. Curiosity has detected plumes of methane gas, which is often a byproduct of living organisms. There is no absolute proof yet, but these discoveries cause many scientists to believe that Mars isn't the barren, dead world we once thought it was.

Many people would like the chance to travel to Mars and live there.

WHY SHOULD WE GO?

The distance from Earth to Mars is enormous: 35 million miles (56 million km) when the planets are closest to each other. A one-way voyage would take at least six to eight months using today's rocket technology. Once on Mars, astronauts will find harsh conditions. It is very cold, there is little oxygen to breathe, dust storms regularly blanket the planet, and harmful radiation from the Sun bombards the surface.

Before we build human colonies on Mars, we have to ask ourselves: what are the reasons for going? Can robotic spacecraft alone do the job? If we send astronauts, why should we risk their lives?

One reason to go is simply to learn. Humans on Mars could perform experiments that would take probes much longer. The more we learn about Mars, the more we learn about planets in general, including Earth. Perhaps something we learn about the Red Planet will help us save our own home world someday.

Another reason to go is economic. Perhaps there are minerals on Mars that are scarce on Earth. Or maybe Mars could be used as a base to mine nearby asteroids.

All the difficulties of getting to Mars can be overcome, but it will take great effort and ingenuity. We have faced similar challenges before. In the 1400s, we knew how to sail, but we couldn't get across the oceans. That changed as technology and our knowledge improved. The same will be true of interplanetary voyages.

A scene from the 2015 movie *The Martian*.

TRAINING FOR MARS

In December 2017, President Donald Trump changed the National Space Policy. As a result, NASA's current plan is to send people to Mars by about 2040. The Moon will first be used to test technology and to set up an outpost. The base will either be the Moon itself, or a Moon-orbiting space station called the Lunar Orbital Platform. It will be similar to today's International Space Station (ISS), but smaller. After the Moon is explored and technology for interplanetary travel has been tested, crewed missions to Mars will begin.

In the coming years, NASA will continue exploring Mars with unmanned orbiters, landers, and rovers. This includes a mission to send samples of Mars rocks to Earth. The technology used to make the return trip will help scientists plan for human expeditions.

NASA is working on a Sample Return Mission that will bring Mars rocks back to Earth for study.

The outside of the NASA HI-SEAS Mars training dome in Hawaii.

A panoramic view of the inside of the HI-SEAS dome.

As new spaceflight technology is built, astronauts will train to live on Mars. NASA's Hawaii Space Exploration Analog and Simulation (HI-SEAS) project tests astronaut psychology. Crews of six volunteers spend up to one year inside a domed habitat. The dome was built on the remote foothills of Hawaii's Mauna Loa volcano. The rocky terrain is similar to what is found on Mars. The volunteers are confined inside the dome, where they eat, sleep, exercise, and work. They eat mostly freeze-dried food, but also grow some of their own vegetables. They sometimes go outside, but only when wearing full spacesuits. NASA hopes to learn how future Mars astronauts will get along with each other during missions that can last years.

GETTING TO MARS

Getting safely to Mars is never easy. About half of all spacecraft sent to the Red Planet have crashed or been sent speeding into deep space by accident. Putting humans inside spacecraft adds another whole level of complexity—and danger.

The biggest problem with sending astronauts from Earth to Mars is the tremendous distance between the two planets. The greater the distance, the longer the trip is going to take.

Mars and Earth are constantly moving around the Sun. Their distance apart is always changing. Earth orbits the Sun once every 365 days. Mars takes about 669 Earth days to finish its orbit. That is a little less than two Earth years. Spacecraft can only begin a trip to Mars when the planets are properly lined up, which happens every 26 months.

When they are closest, Earth and Mars are about 35 million miles (56 million km) apart. However, the actual travel distance a spacecraft must travel is much longer. Because the planets are always moving, a spacecraft follows a long arc to complete the trip. The spacecraft must be aimed where Mars will be at the end of the trip, not where the planet is at launch. (This is like a quarterback passing a football to a running receiver.) Because of this, the spacecraft travels about 300 million total miles (483 million km). That's like taking a one-way trip to the Moon 1,256 times!

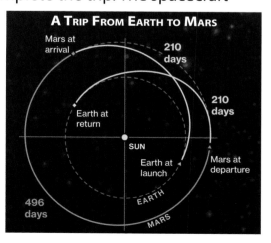

A TRIP FROM EARTH TO MARS

13

A spacecraft passes the Moon on its way to Mars.

Using today's rocket technology, the long voyage to Mars takes seven to eight months. That is a very long time for astronauts to live and work in a cramped space. The long travel time also means astronauts will have to bring much food, and recycle their water and air. If something breaks, they will have to fix it themselves with spare parts they bring.

Making the trip in less time would have many advantages. The crew would need to bring fewer supplies. There would be less time for machinery to break down. It would also mean less time that the crew would be exposed to cancer-causing cosmic rays.

Astronauts train in the cramped quarters of a NASA simulator spacecraft.

The trip to Mars could take less time if a spacecraft could burn more fuel to gain speed. But a mission with a human crew would be many times heavier than a robot probe, especially with all the extra life-support equipment needed. The more weight the spacecraft carries, the more fuel is needed to burn. The extra fuel itself adds even more weight. Bigger rockets with more fuel can be used, but there is a size limit using current technology.

Future spacecraft might use powerful lasers, electromagnetic thrusters, or even nuclear reactors to gain speed. For now, however, NASA will continue to rely on rockets that use chemical reactions to provide thrust. The technology has been used for decades and is dependable. New, faster rocket technology will eventually be used, but it will take time to test and build.

THE ORION SPACECRAFT

O rion is NASA's next generation of manned spacecraft. Named after the constellation in the night sky, Orion will take a crew of four astronauts to the Moon and into deep space. Sometime in the 2030s or 2040s, it will be used to send the first humans to Mars.

For the eight-month voyage to Mars, Orion will include an attached Deep Space Habitat. The bus-sized module is where the four-person crew will live and work safely in deep space. Food, water, and other cargo can also be brought along inside the module.

Besides NASA, private companies are making plans to go into space, and eventually Mars. They include companies such as Boeing, Virgin Galactic, and Blue Origin. SpaceX is a company run by billionaire Elon Musk. In 2017, Musk announced plans to send spacecraft to Mars sometime in the 2020s. His goal is to eventually colonize the Red Planet. That is an ambitious plan, but SpaceX has been very successful so far. Its Falcon-series rockets and Dragon spacecraft have successfully put satellites into Earth orbit and sent supplies to the ISS.

Elon Musk of SpaceX wants to create a spacecraft that could transport people and cargo to Mars in the coming decades.

The Orion Spacecraft

Launch Abort System

This solid rocket system is attached above the Orion crew module. In an emergency, the rocket can fire within milliseconds to quickly propel the astronauts out of harm's way. It then moves to a safe position and drops the crew module for a safe landing. If Orion reaches orbit safely, the launch abort system is discarded.

Crew Module

The Orion crew module is where the four astronauts sit during liftoff and when the capsule returns to Earth. It is similar in appearance to the Apollo spacecraft, but slightly larger. It also has many improved features. They include advanced electronics, navigation, and safety systems. The bottom of the capsule is a heat shield that will protect the crew from the extremely high temperatures of reentry into Earth's atmosphere, which can reach 4,000 degrees Fahrenheit (2,204° C).

Service Module

The service module is a section that attaches to the rear of the crew module. Built with the help of the European Space Agency, it has engine thrusters for navigating through space. The service module also helps the crew survive by providing water, power, air to breathe, and heat. It can also hold cargo that doesn't need to be in the pressurized environment of the crew module. Just before reentry into Earth's atmosphere, the service module is discarded.

Solar Arrays

Four solar arrays unfold after launch.

SPACE LAUNCH SYSTEM

The Orion spacecraft will be sent on its way to Mars by NASA's Space Launch System (SLS). It is the first large rocket system built since the Saturn V rockets, which boosted the Apollo spacecraft to the Moon. The Space Launch System is about the same size as the Saturn V, but provides much more power. It can boost three times as much cargo weight as the space shuttles, which were retired in 2011.

The Space Launch System has three main parts. The central core section is the biggest. It uses four massive engines. They are powered by 730,000 gallons (2.8 million l) of super-cooled liquid oxygen and liquid hydrogen fuel. The fuel is mixed together and ignited.

Two solid rocket boosters are attached to either side of the core rocket. They give extra power that is needed to lift heavy loads into space. Once ignited, the rockets burn 5 tons (4.5 metric tons) of solid fuel per second. When the fuel is spent, the boosters fall away from the core section. When the core reaches orbit, it separates from the Orion spacecraft and falls back to Earth.

Once fully assembled with the Orion spacecraft, the version of the Space Launch System used to launch astronauts to Mars will weigh about 6.5 million pounds (2.9 million kg). That is about the same as 10 fully loaded 747 aircraft. It will be able to lift 286,000 pounds (129,727 kg) of cargo into space, about the same as 22 fully grown elephants. The first version of the Space Launch System and Orion spacecraft will start test flights into space starting in the early 2020s.

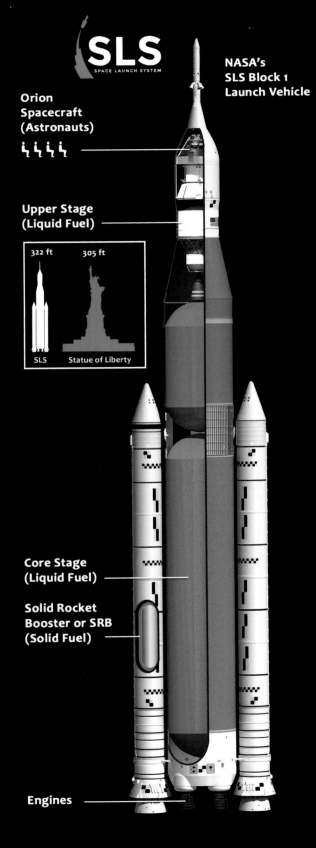

SLS
SPACE LAUNCH SYSTEM

NASA's
SLS Block 1
Launch Vehicle

Orion
Spacecraft
(Astronauts)

Upper Stage
(Liquid Fuel)

322 ft   305 ft

SLS   Statue of Liberty

Core Stage
(Liquid Fuel)

Solid Rocket
Booster or SRB
(Solid Fuel)

Engines

VOYAGE TO MARS

Surviving the eight-month trip to Mars will require a large spacecraft. It will need to carry enough food and water to keep the four-person crew alive. It will also have to carry fuel, shield the astronauts from harmful cosmic radiation, and give them enough room to live comfortably during the long journey. This illustration shows one possible design for a Mars-bound spacecraft.

Propulsion

Spacecraft that use chemical reactions to generate thrust will probably be used on the first interplanetary missions. Some fuel could be made on Mars so the spacecraft wouldn't have to carry a whole round-trip supply. Other options include using nuclear reactors to heat and expel hydrogen, or solar electricity that energizes gasses that create thrust.

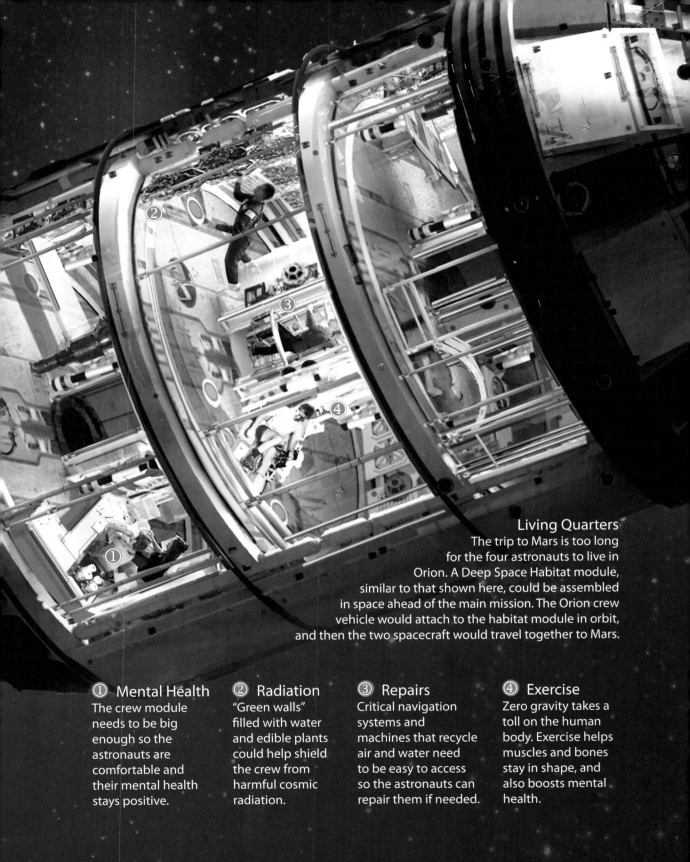

Living Quarters
The trip to Mars is too long for the four astronauts to live in Orion. A Deep Space Habitat module, similar to that shown here, could be assembled in space ahead of the main mission. The Orion crew vehicle would attach to the habitat module in orbit, and then the two spacecraft would travel together to Mars.

① **Mental Health**
The crew module needs to be big enough so the astronauts are comfortable and their mental health stays positive.

② **Radiation**
"Green walls" filled with water and edible plants could help shield the crew from harmful cosmic radiation.

③ **Repairs**
Critical navigation systems and machines that recycle air and water need to be easy to access so the astronauts can repair them if needed.

④ **Exercise**
Zero gravity takes a toll on the human body. Exercise helps muscles and bones stay in shape, and also boosts mental health.

LANDING

When a spacecraft arrives at Mars, it will be traveling many thousands of miles per hour. It needs to slow down somehow. It could reverse its position and fire its engines, but that would use too much fuel. A better option is to use the Martian atmosphere. Even though it is very thin compared to Earth, it is still dense enough to create friction when a fast-moving spacecraft travels through it. The friction will cause the spacecraft to slow down, but will also create scorching heat. The astronauts need to be shielded inside.

After skimming through the upper atmosphere, the spacecraft will slow down and then shoot past Mars. It will go into a wide, elliptical orbit, returning to skim through the atmosphere again and again. Each time, it slows down even more, until it is moving slow enough to go into a circular orbit close to the planet.

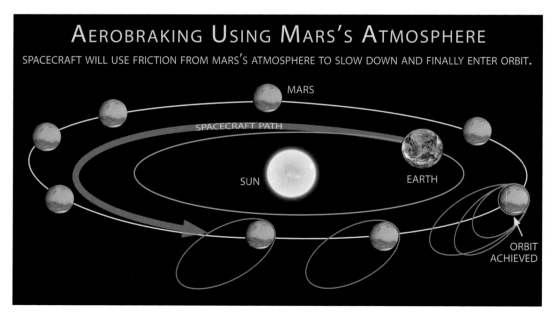

AEROBRAKING USING MARS'S ATMOSPHERE

SPACECRAFT WILL USE FRICTION FROM MARS'S ATMOSPHERE TO SLOW DOWN AND FINALLY ENTER ORBIT.

MARS

SPACECRAFT PATH

SUN

EARTH

ORBIT ACHIEVED

Astronauts will stay safe inside their protective landing vehicle.

Once in a safe orbit, the astronauts will enter a landing vehicle that separates from the main spacecraft. It will protect them from the heat that comes from speeding through the atmosphere. The friction will slow down the landing vehicle, but more help will be needed.

Previous unmanned probes used devices such as airbags to land safely on Mars. Unfortunately, a mission with people and all their supplies will be many times heavier. Old landing methods will not work. A crewed landing vehicle will need parachutes to partially slow down. Then engines will need to fire under the craft so it can land gently. If all goes according to plan, there will be enough fuel left so the astronauts can begin the long journey back home.

LIVING ON MARS

Mars is a hostile place for human beings. The air is too thin. There is almost no oxygen. Sunlight is weak. Temperatures can sink lower than -100 degrees Fahrenheit (-73° C), and cancer-causing solar radiation constantly bombards the dusty surface. If astronauts hope to survive on the Red Planet, they'll have to bring plenty of supplies with them.

Several companies are testing Deep Space Habitats for NASA that could someday be used on Mars. The companies include Bigelow Aerospace, Boeing, and Lockheed Martin. The habitats range from inflatable fabric shelters to hard-sided structures. For use on Mars, the habitats must be pressurized and sealed in order to provide an Earth-like atmosphere and to keep out dust. The walls must shield against solar radiation. The habitats must also have heating and cooling systems, reliable power systems, docking ports, airlocks, and fire safety equipment.

Bigelow Aerospace created an inflatable fabric shelter. One version of this, the Bigelow Expandable Activity Module, was attached to the International Space Station in 2016 for testing and durability.

The first habitat on Mars will likely be transported in several unmanned spacecraft and then assembled on the Red Planet by robots. The human home will be waiting for the first astronauts to arrive.

How much room do astronauts need? That question is more important than it seems. They will be cooped up in one place for many months at a time, with only a few fellow crewmembers for company. After studying astronauts for many years aboard the International Space Station, NASA discovered that astronauts need more room to feel comfortable and productive.

All of these requirements for habitats mean that several trips will probably be needed to get all the required equipment to Mars. Several loads of heavy gear could be sent ahead of time. Perhaps the habitats and other machinery could be assembled by robots. When a human crew arrives, their base camp will be ready and waiting for them.

A BASE ON MARS

Living on Mars will require overcoming many obstacles. There is very little oxygen, temperatures are extremely cold, there is no water on the surface, and gravity is low. Future astronauts will need smart planning, high-tech equipment, and ingenuity to survive.

Nuclear Power
Reliable energy could be created in a small nuclear reactor that splits atoms. A radiation shield would surround the reactor.

NUCLEAR FISSION REACTOR

SOLAR PANELS

Solar Power
Energy from the Sun could make electricity, even though the Sun's rays are weaker on Mars than on Earth.

Lava Tube House
Underground homes inside volcanic lava tubes can help protect against harmful solar radiation.

Oxygen

After running electricity through carbon dioxide that is captured from the Martian atmosphere, the molecules split into oxygen and carbon monoxide. The oxygen can be used to breathe, and the carbon monoxide released back into the Martian atmosphere.

Methane Gas

Carbon dioxide and hydrogen can be combined to form water and methane gas. Methane can be used as rocket fuel.

Water From the Air

The air on Mars is 95 percent carbon dioxide, but it also contains water vapor. A mineral called zeolite absorbs moisture. The water can then be extracted from the zeolite using microwaves.

Groundwater

Microwaves can be used to melt and extract water ice that is found under the Martian surface.

Communication

Messages to and from Earth will be relayed to satellites orbiting Mars.

27

HOW SPACE AFFECTS THE BODY

Spending a long time in space affects the human body in extreme ways. Bones and muscles begin to waste away. Astronauts lose about one percent of their bone

Astronaut Commander Chris Hadfield floats in the International Space Station. NASA scientists are studying the effects of diseases, confinement, isolation, radiation, and gravity fields on human bodies.

mass per month. Regularly lifting weights helps, but not totally. Astronauts often exercise as much as two to four hours a day. Many astronauts also suffer a partial loss of vision. Body fluid collects in the brain while in weightlessness, and the fluid presses on their eyeballs.

After working for months in space, astronauts have a tough time coming back to Earth and dealing with gravity again. Astronaut Chris Hadfield spent nearly five months as commander of the International Space Station (ISS) in 2013. His brain had adjusted to a space environment.

After landing back on Earth, with the full force of gravity now pulling on Hadfield, he became off-balance and sick to his stomach. He had trouble walking. His inner ears, eyes, and brain had to re-adapt to sense which way was up. And even though he had exercised two hours per day on the ISS, his muscles weakened and his bones became more brittle. It took weeks for him to feel better.

NASA scientists fear that when astronauts land on Mars after spending eight months in weightlessness, they will be too sick to perform their mission. Mars has about one-third the gravity of Earth. If astronauts need to spend time in their landing craft getting used to gravity, more air, food, water, and power will need to be brought along. It could be fatal if a disoriented astronaut walked outside too soon and fell, breaking a bone or suffering a concussion.

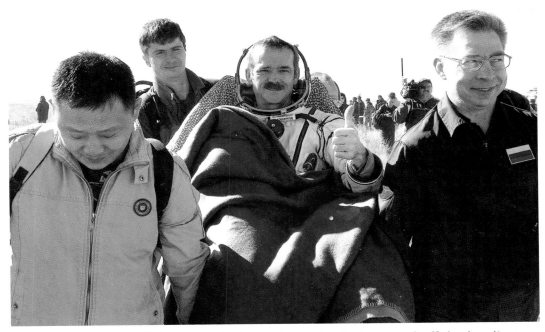

Astronaut Chris Hadfield gives the "thumbs-up" as he's carried off the landing area after returning from the ISS in 2013. He became very sick as his body struggled to adjust to Earth's gravity after nearly five months in space.

Another danger that astronauts will face is radiation. Mars does not have a protective magnetic field surrounding the planet, like Earth. Hazardous cosmic rays and radiation from the Sun constantly bombard the Martian surface. They can harm brain cells, cause radiation sickness, and cause cancer later in life.

Spacecraft and habitats can be shielded with lead, but that makes them too heavy. Walls could possibly be filled with water, which also shields against radiation. Or maybe a device will be invented that makes an artificial magnetic field. New drugs might also help the human body fight off the effects of radiation.

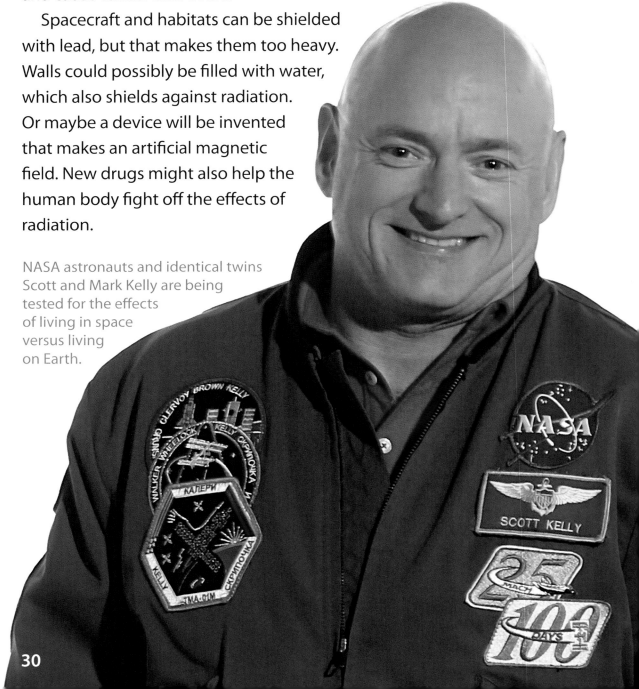

NASA astronauts and identical twins Scott and Mark Kelly are being tested for the effects of living in space versus living on Earth.

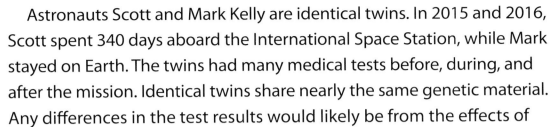

Astronauts Scott and Mark Kelly are identical twins. In 2015 and 2016, Scott spent 340 days aboard the International Space Station, while Mark stayed on Earth. The twins had many medical tests before, during, and after the mission. Identical twins share nearly the same genetic material. Any differences in the test results would likely be from the effects of living in space. NASA especially wanted to know how the human body reacts to weightlessness, radiation, and the mental stress of isolation. Besides coming back to Earth 2 inches (5 cm) taller than his brother (a lack of gravity causes spinal disks to expand— they eventually shrink back to normal), some of Scott Kelly's genes changed. They affected his body's immune system, how his bones form, and how his DNA repairs itself. Many of the changes went back to normal when Kelly returned to Earth, but not all. When doctors finish studying the medical test results, they hope to have a better understanding of the health of future Mars explorers.

SPACESUITS

S pacesuits used by Martian explorers will be different from those used on the space shuttle or the International Space Station, or even those used by the moonwalkers of the Apollo missions. A spacesuit is like a wearable spacecraft. It comes with its own air supply, heating and cooling systems, and radio.

On the hostile surface of Mars, a spacesuit will need a life-support system that lasts long enough for astronauts to complete tasks and experiments that might last for several hours. The suits must be designed for walking on the rocky surface, which means they have to be tough, light, and flexible in the joints, especially the knees, waist, and ankles.

Since the spacesuits used on Mars will be worn for many months, they will need to be very durable. Nobody is sure what kind of fabrics will last the longest in the Martian environment. The Mars 2020 rover will carry fabric samples, including swatches of Teflon and polyurethanes, to see how they wear compared to their durability on Earth.

Spacesuits are evolving. The EMU is used on the ISS. The PXS prototype improves fit and minimizes equipment. The prototype Z-2 is a lightweight, durable suit designed for long missions.

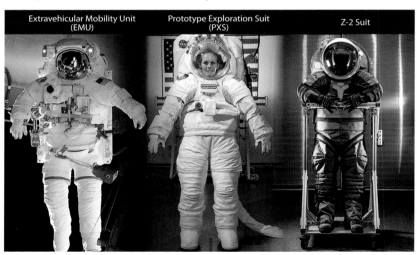

Extravehicular Mobility Unit (EMU) Prototype Exploration Suit (PXS) Z-2 Suit

Engineering professor and former NASA Deputy Administrator Dava Newman has designed a tough, skintight BioSuit that would let astronauts move around easily.

The design of Martian spacesuits could take many forms. It is likely that at first they will look like the bulky, rigid balloon-shaped suits currently used. They look this way because they are filled with pressurized air to simulate the atmospheric pressure on Earth. Other suits might include a more skintight design. These elastic suits apply pressure directly to the skin. Cables and coils "shrink wrap" astronauts into the suit. They would help astronauts be more flexible while they work. These types of suits are still experimental today, but they may be commonplace by the time humans are sent to Mars sometime around 2040.

FINDING WATER

For a yearlong stay on Mars, a crew of astronauts will probably need more water than they can carry from Earth. They will have to use resources found on Mars to survive. Scientists call this "in-situ resource utilization." In-situ means "in its original, natural place."

In the past, scientists believed Mars was a dry, lifeless desert. We now know, thanks to a fleet of Mars orbiters and rovers, that the planet has huge amounts of water. Because of Mars's low atmospheric pressure, liquid water on the surface quickly evaporates. However, there is evidence of vast stores of frozen water under the Martian soil. The polar regions, especially the north pole, are blanketed with water ice. In fact, if all the ice were to suddenly melt, it would flood the entire planet with water 33 feet (10 m) deep.

Getting to the water ice and using it will require special equipment. Microwaves could be used to heat up the soil, and the water vapor could be collected. Water vapor in small amounts is also found naturally in the Martian atmosphere. It is possible to use absorbent materials to capture this water.

Astronauts on Mars may find water by drilling down to get to underground water ice.

GROWING FOOD

Astronauts will have to grow their own food during a long stay on Mars. They will probably not be able to bring enough freeze-dried food with them on the landing ship. For a mission that could last more than a year, fresh food will be important for proper nutrition and variety. Also, plants grown on Mars will convert carbon dioxide to oxygen, just like on Earth.

Growing crops on Mars isn't as simple as it seems. Rays from the Sun are weaker because Mars is millions of miles farther away than Earth. Also, there are chemical differences between Martian and Earth soils. Plants need essential nutrients to grow, including the right amounts of phosphorus, iron, potassium, and nitrogen. These problems might be overcome by using LED light banks inside greenhouses, and by using fertilizers to treat the Martian soil.

Astronauts will have to grow their own fresh food inside specially designed greenhouses on Mars.

Astronauts on the International Space Station grew a crop of "Outredgeous" red romaine lettuce from the Veggie Plant Growth System that tests hardware for growing vegetables and other plants in space.

The crew of a Mars base will probably include someone who knows a lot about botany and biology. In the movie *The Martian*, marooned astronaut Mark Watney was a botanist. His skills helped him survive by growing potatoes in the Martian soil.

Are potatoes really the best crop to grow on Mars? NASA is performing tests aboard the International Space Station to see what kinds of plants can thrive in low gravity and in soil that isn't as fertile as on Earth. Plants such as tomatoes, rye, carrots, and certain herbs, including garden cress, have shown promise.

Heavy stockpiles of rocket fuel will not have to be transported to Mars if it can be made on the Red Planet.

MAKING FUEL

Weight is a critical part of space travel. Heavier loads need more fuel to get to Mars. Fuel itself is heavy, which makes things even more complicated. A heavy spacecraft has to be big just to carry the fuel that will be burned in order to safely land on the surface. That doesn't leave much room for the fuel needed to return to Earth.

If we could somehow make rocket fuel on Mars, we wouldn't have to carry as much, and spaceships could be smaller and lighter. Luckily, Mars has chemicals in abundance that can be converted to rocket fuel.

Mars has frozen water at the poles and underground. The planet's atmosphere contains mostly carbon dioxide. These two resources, when converted by special equipment, can produce oxygen to breathe and rocket fuel.

The first step is to find water ice, melt it, and then run an electric current through it. This process is called electrolysis. The electricity can be provided by solar arrays. The process releases hydrogen for fuel to burn, and oxygen to breathe. Also, hydrogen and oxygen can be combined and used as rocket fuel.

By mixing carbon dioxide in the Martian atmosphere with the hydrogen created by electrolysis, astronauts can create drinking water and methane gas. The methane can be used as rocket fuel. This chemical reaction is called the Sabatier process. It is named after Paul Sabatier, the French chemist who invented it in 1910.

By using these simple chemical reactions, much of the material needed by future Mars explorers will not need to be brought by spacecraft. It will already exist, right there on the planet.

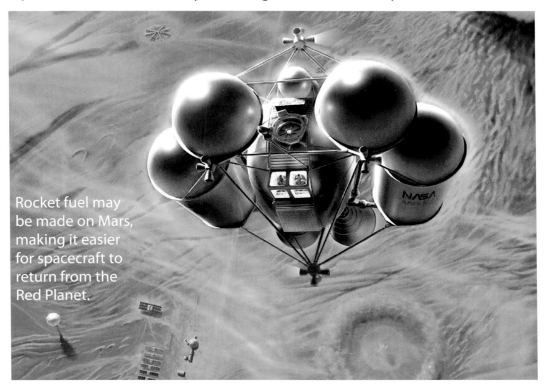

Rocket fuel may be made on Mars, making it easier for spacecraft to return from the Red Planet.

TERRAFORMING MARS

The first humans on Mars will need protective suits.

After exploring Mars and building a large colony, the next step might be to make Mars more like Earth. Right now, if an astronaut were to walk on the surface of Mars without a spacesuit, his or her exposed body fluids, including the linings of the lungs, would start boiling. The atmospheric pressure is too low. Also, there isn't enough oxygen in the Martian air for humans to breathe. Suffocating while one's bodily fluids boil away would be quite unpleasant. Not to mention skin and eyeballs freezing solid when nighttime temperatures drop well below -100 degrees Fahrenheit (-73° C).

The first people to land on Mars will face constant threats to their lives from the Red Planet's harsh environment.

Even though the Martian environment is hostile to humans now, there are good reasons for creating a place other than Earth where people can live. What if a catastrophe wiped out most life on Earth? We know it happened once before when an asteroid killed the dinosaurs. Other disasters might include nuclear war, an incurable virus, or runaway global warming. To avoid humanity's extinction, it might be a good idea to have someplace, a Planet B, where brave pioneers can keep the human race alive.

Of all the planets in our solar system, Mars is the best candidate for being turned into a habitable world like Earth. This process is called terraforming. Right now we don't have all the technology we need to terraform Mars, but that is only a matter of time and determination.

Terraforming Mars will be a long process that could take a few centuries.

How might future astronauts terraform Mars? One plan is to start by increasing the planet's atmospheric pressure. This is important so that liquid water can exist on the surface. There are huge amounts of frozen carbon dioxide at the poles, especially the Martian south pole. During the summer, some of the carbon dioxide ice heats up and turns to gas—a greenhouse gas that thickens the atmosphere and makes the planet warmer. If we could somehow heat up all the polar carbon dioxide ice—perhaps with giant solar mirrors in orbit above the planet—it might make the atmosphere warm and thick enough to support water on the surface. It would take a few centuries, but water ice at the poles and underground would start to flow, flooding the surface with oceans and lakes.

However, the end result might be a "green" Red Planet, capable of supporting life.

Next, humans on Mars would need more oxygen to breathe. Making the soil fertile for plants would help, since plants naturally produce oxygen. Microbes and mosses from Earth, or grown in a lab, could cover the Martian surface. Other plants and trees would follow in the decades to come. Mars would be transformed into a wet, green planet. It would not be a second Earth, but humans could thrive there.

There are many obstacles to exploring Mars. But one thing seems sure, whether we terraform it or not: we will always be fascinated by the Red Planet. It calls to us, that blood-red speck in the night sky. And if we learn enough by studying our sister planet's history, maybe we can use that knowledge to protect and care for the little blue ball in space we call home: Earth.

TIMELINE

Mariner 4

July 14-15, 1965—Mariner 4 (USA) spacecraft, first successful flyby of Mars.

Mariner 9

Nov. 14, 1971—Mariner 9 (USA) orbiter arrives at Mars. First United States spacecraft to orbit a planet other than Earth.

Nov. 27, 1971—Mars 2 (USSR) lander crashes. First human object to reach the surface of Mars.

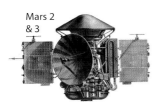
Mars 2 & 3

Dec. 2, 1971—Mars 3 (USSR) lander successfully lands on Mars. Instruments fail 20 seconds after landing.

Viking 1 & 2

July 20, 1976—Viking 1 (USA) lander touches down on Mars. First lander to safely land on Mars and complete its mission.

Sept. 3, 1976—Viking 2 (USA) lander touches down on Mars.

Pathfinder & Sojourner

July 4, 1997—Mars Pathfinder (USA) lands successfully. Sojourner rover begins exploring Mars two days later.

Mars Global Surveyor

Sept. 11, 1997—Mars Global Surveyor (USA) begins polar orbit around Mars and starts a nine-year mapping mission.

Oct. 24, 2001—Mars Odyssey (USA) orbiter reaches Mars. Studies Mars's geology and radiation, and acts as communications relay for Martian rovers.

Dec. 25, 2003—Mars Express (European Space Agency) spacecraft enters Mars orbit. Accompanying Beagle 2 rover crashes on surface.

Jan. 4, 2004—Spirit (USA) rover lands on Mars.

Jan. 25, 2004—Opportunity (USA) rover lands on Mars.

March 10, 2006—Mars Reconnaissance Orbiter (USA) reaches Mars.

May 25, 2008—Phoenix (USA) lander arrives at the Martian north pole, verifies presence of water ice.

August 6, 2012—Mars Science Laboratory (USA) rover, nicknamed Curiosity, lands on Mars.

Sept. 22, 2014—MAVEN (USA) orbiter reaches Mars and studies the Red Planet's upper atmosphere.

Sept. 24, 2014—Mars Orbiter Mission (India), also called *Mangalyaan* (Hindi for "Mars Craft"), reaches Mars and begins studying the planet's atmosphere. It is India's first mission to Mars.

Oct. 19, 2016—ExoMars Trace Gas Orbiter (joint European Space Agency and Roscosmos (Russia)) enters orbit around Mars. Lander crashes.

GLOSSARY

ASTEROID
A rocky object, smaller than a planet, that revolves around the Sun, usually between the orbits of Mars and Jupiter. Their size ranges from one to several hundred miles in diameter. Mars's two moons, Phobos and Deimos, are probably asteroids captured by the planet's gravitational pull millions of years ago.

COSMIC RAYS
High-energy radiation that usually comes from outside the Solar System, possibly from the supernova of stars in our galaxy, or even from other galaxies. Without the protection of Earth's atmosphere, astronauts that are exposed to this radiation can be stricken with cancer.

INTERPLANETARY
Located or traveling between the planets of a solar system.

MICROBE
Small lifeforms (microorganisms), such as bacteria, fungi, or viruses. The Curiosity rover's main mission was to explore whether Mars could be home to microbial life in its distant past.

NATIONAL AERONAUTICS AND SPACE ADMINISTRATION (NASA)
A United States government space agency started in 1958. NASA's goals include space exploration, as well as increasing people's understanding of Earth, our solar system, and the universe.

NATIONAL SPACE POLICY
A set of rules and goals for the space program of the United States. It is set by the president, with advice from science and industry experts. It is then approved and funded by Congress.

ORBIT

The circular path a moon or spacecraft makes when traveling around a planet or other large celestial body. There are several satellites orbiting Mars, including NASA's Mars Reconnaissance Orbiter and the European Space Agency's ExoMars Trace Gas Orbiter.

PROBE

An unmanned space vehicle that is sent on missions that are too dangerous, or would take too long, for human astronauts to accomplish. Probes are equipped with many scientific instruments, like cameras and radiation detectors. Information from these instruments is radioed back to ground controllers on Earth.

ROVER

A robotic vehicle that is driven over rough terrain by remote control.

TERRAFORM

Modifying a planet on purpose to make its atmosphere, temperature, and ecology similar to Earth's. The dream of some scientists is to terraform Mars so that large populations of colonists from Earth can someday live on the Red Planet.

ONLINE RESOURCES

Booklinks
NONFICTION NETWORK
FREE! ONLINE NONFICTION RESOURCES

To learn more about humans to Mars, visit abdobooklinks.com. These links are routinely monitored and updated to provide the most current information available.

INDEX